The
Mayo Brothers' Heritage

Quotes & Pictures

Thomas M. Habermann, M.D.

Renee E. Ziemer

Carolyn Stickney Beck, Ph.D.

Mayo Clinic Scientific Press

Rochester, Minnesota

Mayo Clinic Scientific Press, 200 1st St SW,
Rochester, Minnesota 55905

Printed in the USA

ISBN 1-893005-91-7

10 9 8 7 6 5 4 3 2 1

Foreword

The two words "Mayo Clinic" are perhaps the most recognized name in health care in the world today. This recognition has resulted in nearly a century of interactions with several generations of patients who have told friends, family, and others of their experiences. A key attribute to Mayo Clinic health care is that of keeping the individual patient and his or her family as the central focus of our activities. This attribute is directly related to the constancy of our primary value—"the needs of the patient come first"—despite astounding social change. Mayo Clinic has maintained this value over the years by keeping one eye on tradition, one eye on the future, and our feet in the present. The collection of quotes and photographs in this monograph vivifies how our predecessors at Mayo Clinic respected and valued their past, concentrated their energies on the present, and consistently looked to the future. What comes through in the text and photographs is a legacy of outstanding leadership in the medical profession. I expect that readers of this book for decades to come will appreciate the vision and values of the Mayo Clinic that have brought us to where we are today.

Michael B. Wood, M.D.
President and Chief Executive Officer
Mayo Foundation

Preface

Like a patient's history, the history of Mayo Clinic most often appears to us in fragments, not necessarily in chronological or categorical order. Patient service representatives, clinical assistants, supportive ancillary staff, paramedical personnel, secretaries, nurses, administrators, clergy, clinical associates, research associates, master's-level researchers, Ph.D.-level staff, medical students, residents, fellows, faculty, and faculty physicians are all responsible for discovering patterns in the fragments of information about a patient. This information ranges from personal and family history to actual features of the human genome. In time, we are able to interpret these patterns in broad frameworks as we engage in education and research. Even in these broad frameworks, our ongoing concern is caring for patients.

The Mayo Clinic evolved from the medical practice of Dr. William Worrall Mayo and his two sons, Dr. William James Mayo and Dr. Charles Horace Mayo.

In preparing this publication, we reviewed the collected papers and other excerpts of Dr. William J. Mayo and Dr. Charles H. Mayo. In this review, we discovered that many familiar quotations reveal even greater insight within the fuller context of statements. Also, many previously unpublished photographs reveal the depth and nuances of the Mayo brothers.

We first presented this collection of images and text for the Department of Medicine Grand Rounds as a program for Mayo Clinic Heritage Days in October 2000. As in that presentation, the excerpts in this book focus on practice and education and are presented in more or less chronological order. There is not necessarily chronological congruence between each photograph and its associated excerpt. Instead, our pairing of photographs and excerpts reflects our interpretation of the spirit of the words and images. Where possible, we have included citations and dates to orient the reader chronologically. The quotations are unaltered from their original wording. Thus, some of the language may not meet current standards of inclusiveness. We hope readers understand our goal of accuracy.

Patients and colleagues have taught us repeatedly that it is an enormous responsibility and privilege to care for and with others day by day. As we reflect on the development of this book, we are mindful of how the previous millennium is unfolding into the new millennium. Perhaps the blueprint of the Doctors Mayo is more sustainable than we have anticipated. If this book has caused you to think, then it has accomplished its task.

Thomas M. Habermann, M.D.
Renee E. Ziemer
Carolyn Stickney Beck, Ph.D.

Acknowledgments

I would like to acknowledge the remarkable help given to me to develop this book. My parents, Audrey and Jim, provided an example and opportunity. As a physician, my father initially referred patients to Mayo Clinic as a general practitioner and then sent tissue slides as a pathologist to Mayo Clinic. I thank my wife, Mary Jo, for her support. Renee Ziemer of the Mayo Clinic Historical Unit gathered the photographs, helped to date the photographs, helped find quotations, and proofread the references. The leadership of Carolyn Stickney Beck, Ph.D., Mayo Center for Humanities in Medicine, allowed the project and its multiple facets to proceed. Carolyn Johnston helped to assemble the original presentation. Mary Ellen Landwehr was an invaluable sounding board from the beginning of the project. The following individuals, from Media Support Services, assisted in reproducing the photographs: Sandra Borgschatz, Peggy Chihak, Nichole Crawley, Sandra Gaspar, JoLee Gruber, Kristi Hunter, Lisa Oeltjen, Nikki Olson-Nietz, Rhonda Rosburg, and Karen Sprenger. We are grateful for the efforts of Marianne Hockema, secretary of the Medical/Industry Relations Committee. We are most indebted to Jeffrey Satre for his work in designing the book and to Jon Bedsted for his assistance with the printing of the book. A special thanks to LeAnn Stee and Roberta Schwartz in the Section of Scientific Publications; they provided editorial assistance, encouragement, and advice at key times. We are grateful to Dr. Joseph G. Murphy, Chair of the Section of Scientific Publications, for his support. Sharon Wadleigh verified the quotations and credit lines and did the keyboarding, and Kenna Atherton provided expert proofreading. Lastly, I appreciate the understanding and support of my family.

Thomas M. Habermann, M.D.
*Consultant, Division of Hematology
and Internal Medicine, Mayo Clinic
Professor of Medicine, Mayo Medical School*

Reprint books of Dr. William J. Mayo (top) and Dr. Charles H. Mayo (bottom) photographed in their offices on the third floor of the Plummer Building

Dr. Charles H. Mayo, Dr. William W. Mayo, and Dr. William J. Mayo, circa 1890

"No one is big enough to be independent of others."

A quote by Dr. William W. Mayo referred to in Clapesattle H. *The Doctors Mayo*. Minneapolis: The University of Minnesota Press, 1941, pages 534-535.

Dr. Charles H. Mayo, 1921

On November 18, 1933, a doctor from San Diego, California, having read comments by Dr. William Mayo about his brother, Dr. Charles Mayo, wrote Dr. Will to describe an encounter he had had with Dr. Charlie in 1901 or 1902.

"...I was again reminded of an experience I had over 30 years ago which showed the type of man [Dr. Charlie] is ...I was an interne [sic].... The attending man ...did a ...hysterectomy.... When closing, I called his attention to bleeding...but he [the attending] said it was alright and closed the abdomen...."

"That night ...the patient showed definite signs of intra-abdominal hemorrhage and I called [the attending] at his home....He arrived, accompanied by 5 or 6 physicians....[He] said, 'Well, go ahead and operate.' ...This done, the attending man asked if I could get along alright ...and he left accompanied by all but one of the original group."

"I thought to myself that the remaining doctor was probably a man come in from down in the State anxious to learn what he could from an interne [sic] but each time that I looked at him and caught his bright, clear eyes, which I can see to this day, I was more certain that he was not an ordinary country doctor. He remained in the room watching me until the last skin suture was in and then he thanked me and left."

"The next morning while in ...Clinic I saw the same pair of bright eyes in the doorway and as he came in, [one of the attendings] called 'Hello Charlie Mayo, when did you come to town.' ...Here he was visiting ...for a few hours, came to ...Hospital as a guest after his dinner, saw a patient that needed expert care turned over to a senior Interne [sic] and when the operator left remained in case his advice might help save the patient's life."

According to a letter written in November 1933.

In 1922, while visiting President Obregon in Mexico City, Dr. William J. Mayo was invited to attend a bullfight as the president's guest. During the bullfight, a young bullfighter was gored by a bull.

"President Obregon asked Dr. Mayo to see whether he could do anything to save the young man."

"The ease and speed with which he stopped the hemorrhage made a tremendous impression on the watching group, and word somehow got back to the crowd in the ring, so that when Dr. Will returned to his seat he was given a prolonged ovation."

Clapesattle H. *The Doctors Mayo*. Minneapolis: The University of Minnesota Press, 1941, pages 585-587.

Dr. William J. Mayo, upper right corner of photograph, returning to his seat after attending an injured bullfighter in Mexico City in 1922

Dr. William J. Mayo, date of photograph unknown

"…Graduating Class of the Medical Department …1895"

"Above all things, let me urge upon you the absolute necessity of careful examinations for the purpose of diagnosis. My own experience has been that the public will forgive you an error in treatment more readily than one in diagnosis, and I fully believe that more than one-half of the failures in diagnosis are due to hasty and unmethodic examinations."

Mayo WJ. Address delivered to the graduating class of the Medical Department of the Minnesota State University, Minneapolis, Minnesota, May 5, 1895. *Northwestern Lancet* 1895;15:221-224.

"…careful examination …"

"Do this in every case."

"The mental effect on the patient is good, the practical knowledge to yourself is better, and if you avail yourselves of all the means of physical diagnosis and repeated examinations, the number of unsolved cases will be surprisingly small."

Mayo WJ. Address delivered to the graduating class of the Medical Department of the Minnesota State University, Minneapolis, Minnesota, May 5, 1895. *Northwestern Lancet* 1895;15:221-224.

Dr. William J. Mayo, date of photograph unknown

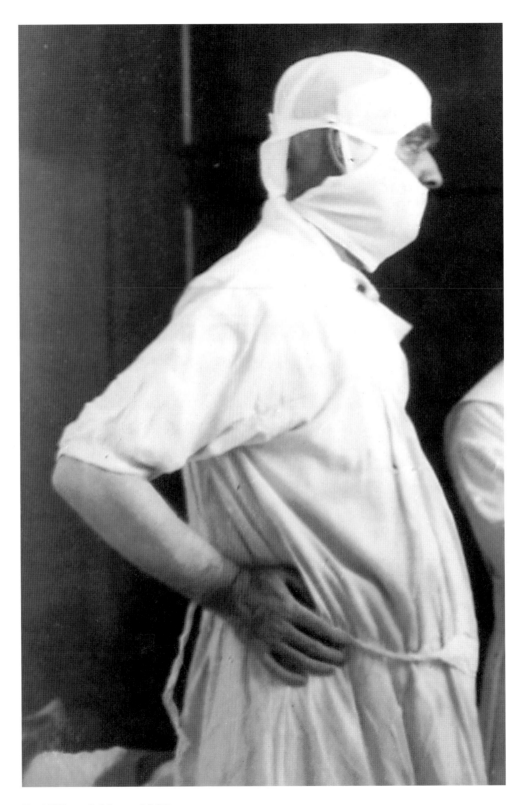

Dr. William J. Mayo, 1915

"What are the rewards of so laborious a life?"

"They can not be measured, because there is no standard of comparison. To realize that one has devoted himself to the most holy of all callings, that without thought of reward he has alleviated the sufferings of the sick and added to the length and usefulness of human life, is a source of satisfaction money can not buy."

Mayo WJ. The medical profession and the issues which confront it. *JAMA* 1906;46:1737-1740.

Dr. William J. Mayo and Dr. Charles H. Mayo, circa 1910

Rush Medical College Commencement Address

"Errors of judgment in student days were made harmless by the care and attention of your teachers. From now on you will have no such check upon your actions, and your mistakes will be costly because they concern the health and happiness, if not the life, of individuals."

"As we have become more and more dependent upon the laboratory and special investigations in making our diagnosis, we have gradually lost that faculty of clinical observation which enabled these early clinicians to make an accurate diagnosis in the more common diseases almost with a glance at the patient."

Mayo WJ. The necessity of cooperation in the practice of medicine. *Collected Papers by the Staff of Saint Mary's Hospital, Mayo Clinic* 1910;2:557-566.

"Cultivate methodic habits of study."

"I would suggest the plan of reading not less than one hour a day."

"Never allow yourself to borrow from the future."

"Write papers; they will do you much good, although at first they may not benefit any one else."

"Attend your medical societies...."

"I would admonish you, above all other considerations, to be honest. I mean honesty in every conception of the word: let it enter into all the details of your work; in the treatment of your patients and in your association with your brother practitioners."

Mayo WJ. The necessity of cooperation in the practice of medicine.
Collected Papers by the Staff of Saint Mary's Hospital, Mayo Clinic 1910;2:557-566.

Dr. William J. Mayo, circa 1905

Dr. Charles H. Mayo and Dr. William J. Mayo, 1915

"There is but one answer to the question,—coöperation in medicine."

"Medicine must no longer be practiced individually, but by groups of men, each one bringing the results of his work and studies to bear upon the case. In no other way can the patient receive the benefits to which he is entitled. How this coöperation can be satisfactorily brought about is our present problem."

Mayo WJ. Contributions of the nineteenth century to a living pathology. *Boston Med Surg J* 1912;167:751-754.

Dr. Charles H. Mayo, circa 1908

"To keep a patient in the hospital longer than is necessary is an unwarranted expense to him or an unjustified tax on those who contribute to hospital expenses, besides keeping some other needy patient from being cared for."

Mayo CH. The hospital as an educational institution. *Mod Hosp* 1914;3:215-218.

Dr. William J. Mayo, 1918

"I have always thought a good deal of Lincoln's Gettysburg address. There's a line in it which explains why we want to do this thing. It is 'that these dead shall not have died in vain.' We know how hard it is for those who have had the misfortune of deaths in their families, of deaths that might have been avoided. What better could we do than take young men and help them become proficient in the profession so as to prevent needless deaths?"

Foundation life goal, Dr. William J. Mayo tells senators. *Minneapolis Morning Tribune*, March 23, 1917.

"Science and education have done much but education still lags."

Mayo CH. The relation of mouth conditions to general health. *J Natl Dent Assoc* 1919;6:505-512.

Dr. Charles H. Mayo, circa 1918

Dr. William J. Mayo, 1916

"The medical profession is grouping itself along scientific lines, not for the profit of the doctor, but in order that he may more adequately and satisfactorily perform his work. This will give patients the benefit of modern medical knowledge."

Mayo WJ. Socialization of medicine and of law. Presented before the joint meeting of the Wisconsin and Minnesota State Bar Associations, La Crosse, Wisconsin, July, 1919.

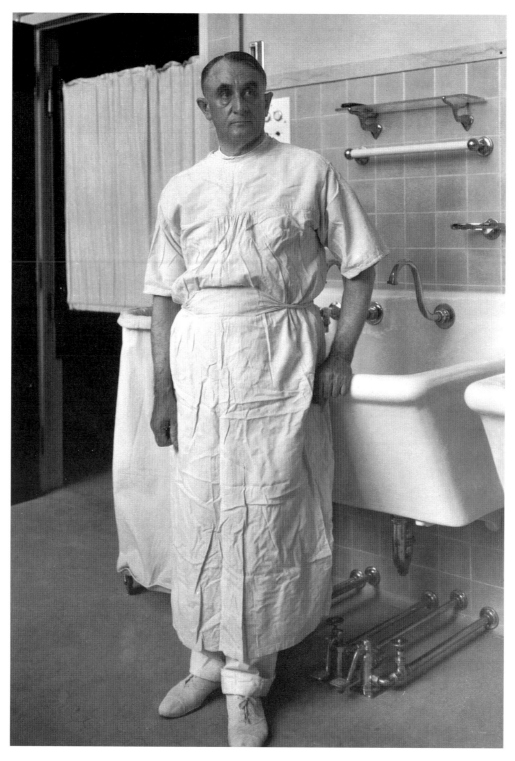

Dr. Charles H. Mayo in the 1920s

"It must be remembered that physicians of today are trained to treat the sick and they must learn how to examine so-called well persons to prevent them from getting sick."

Mayo CH. The relation of anatomy to present-day surgery.
JAMA 1920;74:367-369.

"On every side we see the acceptance of an idea which is generally expressed by the loose term 'group medicine,' a term which fails in many respects to express conditions clearly. In my father's time success in the professions was more or less dependent on convention, tradition, and impressive surroundings. The top hat and the double-breasted frock coat of the doctor, the wig and gown of the jurist, and the clerical garb of the ecclesiastic, supplied the necessary stage scenery."

Mayo WJ. The medical profession and the public. *JAMA* 1921;75:921-925.

Dr. William J. Mayo, date of photograph unknown

"So tremendous has been the recent advance of medicine that no one man can understand more than a small fraction of it; thus, physicians have become more or less dependent on the skill, ability, and specialized training of other physicians for sufficient knowledge to care for the patient intelligently."

Mayo WJ. The medical profession and the public. *JAMA* 1921;76:921-925.

Dr. William J. Mayo, circa 1938-1939

Dr. William J. Mayo, date of photograph unknown

"It is well for America that the medical profession has recognized the necessity for organized scientific effort which is taking the place of former competitive medicine. Competitive medicine was the response of the individual physician to his training and environment."

Mayo WJ. The medical profession and the public. *JAMA* 1921;76:921-925.

Dr. William J. Mayo, date of photograph unknown

"The organization of departments of trained workers in special fields of medicine and allied sciences greatly aids in obtaining knowledge which permits a better interpretation of all the facts of the case by the diagnostician and brings knowledge closer to treatment. We can hope that eventually knowledge will precede treatment and that treatment will be based on knowledge, and not, as heretofore, largely on empiricism."

Mayo WJ. The medical profession and the public. *JAMA* 1921;76:921-925.

"The medical profession can be the greatest factor for good in America. The greatest asset of a nation is the health of its people."

Mayo WJ. The medical profession and the public. *JAMA* 1921;76:921-925.

Dr. William J. Mayo, 1915 or 1916

Dr. William J. Mayo, 1922

"Medicine's place is fixed by its services to mankind; if we fail to measure up to our opportunity it means state medicine, political control, mediocrity, and loss of professional ideals."

Mayo WJ. The medical profession and the public. *JAMA* 1921;76:921-925.

"Experience is the great teacher; unfortunately, experience leaves mental scars, and scar tissue contracts."

Mayo WJ. In the time of Henry Jacob Bigelow. *JAMA* 1921;77:597-603.

Dr. William J. Mayo, circa 1918

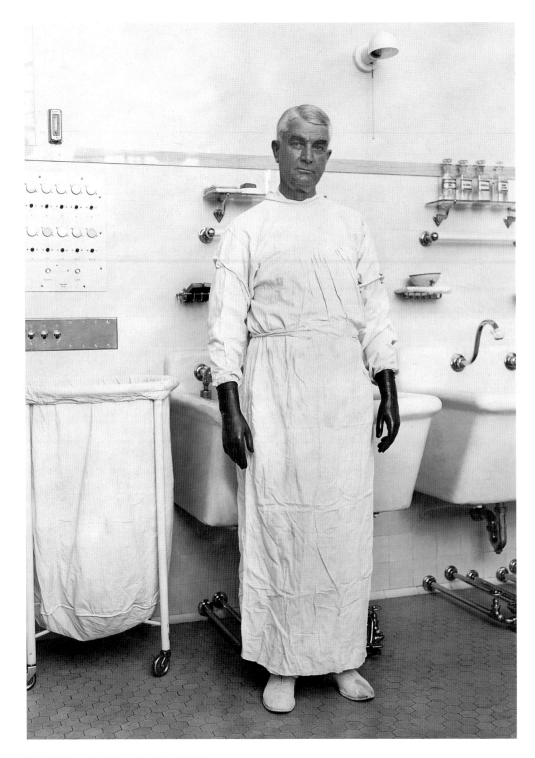

Dr. William J. Mayo in the 1920s

"The internist, the surgeon, and the specialist must join with the physiologists, the pathologists, and the laboratory workers to form the clinical group which must also include men learned in the abstract sciences...."

Mayo WJ. The medical profession and the public. *JAMA* 1921;76:921-925.

1914 Building (left) and Plummer Building (center)

"As I have previously pointed out, a medical building with a medical library where physicians can meet, common access to laboratories containing modern means of diagnosis with good technicians in charge, the whole managed and controlled by the physicians of a community, would enable every patient, rich or poor, to obtain proper treatment."

Mayo WJ. The medical profession and the public. *JAMA* 1921;76:921-925.

*"The ills of today do not cloud
the horizon of tomorrow."*

Mayo WJ. The function of the university concerns the
tomorrows, the function of the government,
the yesterdays and todays. Read before the Alumni
Association of Harvard University Medical School,
Boston, June 19, 1924.

Dr. William J. Mayo, date of photograph unknown

Dr. William J. Mayo, 1923

"A few years ago we realized our possibilities in the Clinic for higher medical education."

"The future of the Clinic lies with the young men."

"The Clinic should be prepared to lose its best men."

"Specialization has come to stay."

"Specialization has brought revolutionary results in many fields of medicine."

"In the Clinic, the small groups within the big group have been particularly important."

Mayo WJ. The future of the clinic. *Tr A Resid & Ex-Resid Physicians, Mayo Clin* 1924;5:121-124.

"Doctors who work alone, as most do, are unfortunately individualists. Few of them develop that respect for the other fellow's opinion which teamwork and group medicine engender."

Mayo CH. Address of the president delivered at the convocation of the American College of Surgeons. *Surg Gynecol Obstet* 1925;40:447-448.

Dr. Charles H. Mayo, circa 1925

Dr. William J. Mayo and Dr. Charles H. Mayo, 1925

"I remember …when the name of doctor, in this country, did not carry much weight. Medical education was then in the hands of clinical men. Men were taught, as doctors, to care for sick people.…But as time has gone on the amount of knowledge has become so great …and during this time there has been a change in the whole tone of education.…"

Mayo WJ. Medical education. *Tr A Resid & Ex-Resid Physicians, Mayo Clin* 1925;6:285-287.

"The high purpose of true medical education is to fit the student to think in medicine; in fact, it can be said that education is a failure in that degree that it fails to train the student to reason and develop judgment as he acquires knowledge of disease and treatment and prevention as applied to the individual case."

Mayo CH. Problems in medical education. *Collected Papers of The Mayo Clinic and The Mayo Foundation* 1926;1093-1102.

Dr. Charles H. Mayo, date of photograph unknown

Dr. Charles H. Mayo speaks to the students of the London Hospital Medical College and Dental School, 1925

"The educational product, of necessity, will be, as it has always been, dependent on the ability of its instructors and teachers to inspire and the capacity of its students to emulate. The study of medicine and dentistry but plants the roots of knowledge; it does not make brains, but merely molds them and equips them for more and greater work."

Mayo CH. Problems in medical education. *Collected Papers of The Mayo Clinic and The Mayo Foundation* 1926;1093-1102.

"There are two objects of medical education: to heal the sick, and to advance the science....Medicine is both an art and a science, and both make appeal to the true physician."

Mayo CH. Problems in medical education. *Collected Papers of The Mayo Clinic and The Mayo Foundation* 1926;1093-1102.

Dr. Charles H. Mayo, 1925

Dr. Charles H. Mayo and Dr. William J. Mayo, 1921

"Today we are suffering from too much knowledge too widely diffused....Without intending to criticize unkindly, I believe that we devote too much effort to driving home detailed information and too little to the development of perspective."

Mayo WJ. Medical education for the general practitioner.
JAMA 1927;88:1377-1379.

"It has been said, and I believe justly, that one should go to the educator for information but not for advice. This is especially true in medical education. The actual practice of medicine must be taught by example as well as by precept."

Mayo WJ. Medical education for the general practitioner.
JAMA 1927;88:1377-1379.

Dr. William J. Mayo, 1933

Dr. William J. Mayo and Dr. Charles H. Mayo, 1925

"Medical cooperation is essential if the people are to have the benefit of modern medical knowledge. Unfortunately, group medicine has caught the eye of the profession too much on the financial side to the subordination of the professional side."

Mayo WJ. Medical education for the general practitioner.
JAMA 1927;88:1377-1379.

Dr. William J. Mayo, 1930

"The glory of medicine is that it is constantly moving forward, that there is always more to learn. The ills of today do not cloud the horizon of tomorrow, but act as a spur to greater effort."

Mayo WJ. The aims and ideals of the American Medical Association. *J Nat Education A* 1928;158-163.

"We must bear in mind the difference between thoroughness and efficiency. Thoroughness gathers all the facts, but efficiency distinguishes the two-cent pieces of non-essential data from the twenty dollar gold pieces of fundamental fact."

Mayo WJ. Looking backward and forward in medical education. Paper presented at the dedication of the new Medical Plant of the University of Iowa, Iowa City, Iowa, November 15, 1928 and published in *J Iowa State Med Soc* 1929;19:41-46.

Dr. William J. Mayo, 1933

Dr. Charles H. Mayo, date of photograph unknown

"Their clinical observations were often strikingly accurate...."

"Yet they called themselves modern and looked back at their predecessors with a patronizing sort of pity from the pinnacles of scientific success to which they had attained....I cannot always be sure that a century from now somebody will not be saying the same sort of thing about us."

"Perhaps somebody may run across these lines in fifty or a hundred years and comment with tolerant pity: 'Well, he had a glimmering of vision, anyway!'"

"I believe we are traveling the road to the elucidation of all disease, but the journey's end may be a long way off."

"Thus the specialist's practice exacts wider knowledge of the body in health and disease; he must be able to examine the entire body...."

"At the same time the increasing intricacy ...tends to make him subdivide his specialty ...to 'know more and more about less and less.'"

Mayo CH. Medicine in retrospect. *Ann Otol Rhinol Laryngol* 1928;37:206-208.

Dr. William J. Mayo and Dr. Charles H. Mayo, date of photograph unknown

"The educator has assumed almost full charge of medical education."

Mayo WJ. Looking backward and forward in medical education. Paper presented at the dedication of the new Medical Plant of the University of Iowa, Iowa City, Iowa, November 15, 1928 and published in *J Iowa State Med Soc* 1929;19:41-46.

Dr. Charles H. Mayo, date of photograph unknown

"Probably in the not far distant future we will crawl out of our old methods of education, as a snake sheds its skin, and reorganize a new plan."

Mayo CH. Educational development of man. *Collected Papers of The Mayo Clinic and The Mayo Foundation* 1928;20:937-942.

"How fortunate we have been who have lived during this great period of medical progress of say, thirty years, yet I have heard my father say the same, many years ago."

Mayo CH. Medicine in retrospect. *Ann Otol Rhinol Laryngol* 1928;37:206-208.

Dr. William J. Mayo, Dr. William W. Mayo, and Dr. Charles H. Mayo, 1905

Dr. Charles H. Mayo, date of photograph unknown

"What a privilege it is to be able to teach, and how comparatively few of the many who possess the knowledge to teach are able to impart it to the student in a manner to make a permanent rather than a fleeting impression on his mind, and at the same time arouse interest."

Mayo CH. Educational development of man. *Collected Papers of The Mayo Clinic and The Mayo Foundation* 1928;20:937-942.

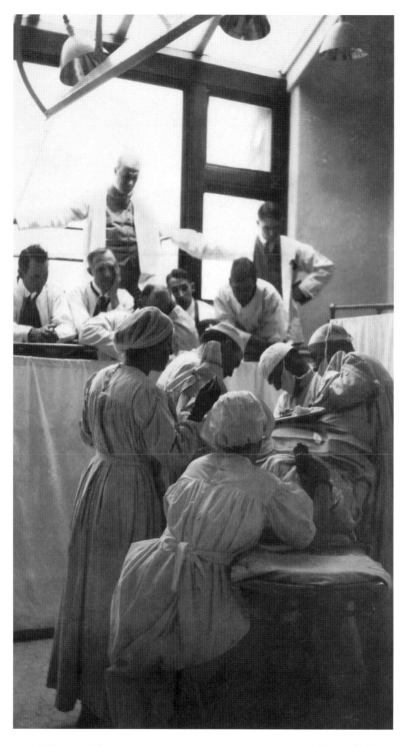

Dr. William J. Mayo (second masked person on the right), 1913

"I can visualize the older men among us, those who have passed middle age, standing at a half-opened door. They see the young men who will carry forward beyond our time, and beyond them, still other young men who will take their places when they are gone. As time goes on, the Clinic will be justified by the good it has done."

Mayo WJ. The future of the clinic. *Tr A Resid & Ex-Resid Physicians, Mayo Clin* 1924;5:121-124.

"Medicine is a profession for social service and it developed organization in response to social need."

Mayo CH. International medical progress. *Collected Papers of The Mayo Clinic and The Mayo Foundation* 1931;23:1020-1024.

Dr. Charles H. Mayo purchasing Christmas Seals, date of photograph unknown

1928 Plummer Building

"As I think of the many years of work for a great cause, I like to believe that the whole structure of the Clinic is that of an institution engaged in research in medical education, social and practical as well as scientific."

"Research in education, for improved curricula, so that education may more nearly fit its purpose, is as necessary as research in any other field."

"Each day as I go through the hospitals surrounded by younger men, they give me of their dreams and I give them of my experience, and I get the better of the exchange."

Mayo WJ. Remarks. *Proc Staff Meet Mayo Clin* 1931;6:591-593.

"One meets with many men who have been fine students, and who have stood high in their classes, who have great knowledge of medicine but very little wisdom in application. They have mastered the science, and have failed in the understanding of the human being."

Mayo WJ. The preliminary education of the clinical specialist. *Collected Papers of The Mayo Clinic and The Mayo Foundation* 1931;23:1001-1005.

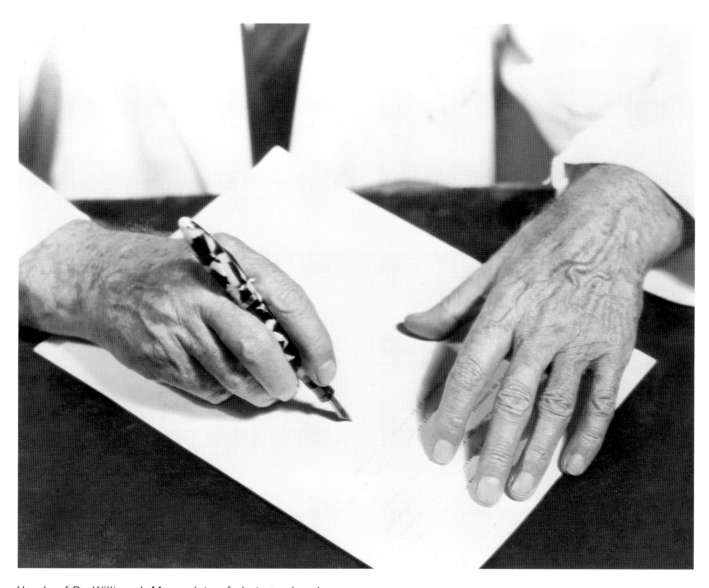

Hands of Dr. William J. Mayo, date of photograph unknown

Dr. Charles H. Mayo, date of photograph unknown

"Today the only thing that is permanent is change."

"The physical, chemical, philosophical, medical and educational systems which served us so well a quarter of a century ago are largely being superseded and relegated to the pages of history of progress."

"It took the world from the day of its creation to the time of the sixteenth century to raise a doubting Thomas of sufficient mental strength and courage to state that questions were answered not by authority, but by experiment."

"The great contribution we can make is to prepare the oncoming generations to think that they can and will think for themselves."

Mayo CH. Tomorrow's education seen by Dr. Mayo. *Northwestern Univ Alumni News* 1931;10:17-19.

Dr. William J. Mayo, 1934

"…success in the practice of medicine depends to a large extent on the understanding of human emotions.…"

"Because of greater comprehension of the emotions there has come about …the removal of a piece of tissue for microscopic examination …before performing a disfiguring operation."

"Prolongation of life must come first, and comfort and emotional stability second.…"

"Perhaps there is no better summing up of the duty of the physician to the patient than the Golden Rule.…"

"…one finds that success depends more on the imponderables than on those things which can be weighed and measured."

Mayo WJ. The social training of the surgeon and physician. *Proc Staff Meet Mayo Clin* 1932;7:193-197.

"I well remember my first visit as a young man to Hopkins. I arrived at the hospital one morning and wandered around through the building devoted to reception. A quickly moving gentleman with a small mustache came into the building, stepped up to me, and said, 'Well, what would you like to see?'"

"I replied, 'I am a young doctor from the West and I have heard so much about this hospital that I should like to visit it, if I am not in the way.'"

"He introduced himself as Dr. Osler...."

"In this way I became acquainted with Dr. Osler, and I afterward had occasion to meet him often. He always remembered me, he always was interested in what I was doing, and, as the years went by, from various places in foreign countries he sent little mementos [sic], usually something about brothers."

"...the fact that he was great because he loved his fellow man. His teaching was concerned always with the desire to understand better, in order to do more for the sick human being."

"For the influence of Hopkins is due to more than fine teachers and outstanding clinicians. The joining of all forces for good into a compact organization has required wisdom and humanitarianism which the history of medicine has seldom shown."

Mayo WJ. What we owe to Johns Hopkins University. *Proc Staff Meet Mayo Clin* 1932;7:32-34.

Sir William Osler, date of photograph unknown

Dr. William J. Mayo purchasing a poppy on Poppy Sale Day, 1935

"One of the chief defects in our plan of education in this country is that we give too much attention to developing the memory and too little to developing the mind; we lay too much stress on acquiring knowledge and too little on the wise application of knowledge."

Mayo WJ. The economic relation of the university system to the development of a social democracy. *Collected Papers of The Mayo Clinic and The Mayo Foundation* 1933;25:1105-1107.

Dr. Charles H. Mayo and Dr. William J. Mayo, 1935

"The fine relationship between the physician and the patient and the patient's family and friends existed much more closely in the days of our fathers than today."

Mayo WJ. The value of the imponderables in clinical medicine. Proceedings of the Inter-State Postgraduate Medical Assembly of North America, Cleveland, Ohio, October 16-21, 1933.

"The best interest of the patient is the only interest to be considered, and in order that the sick may have the benefit of advancing knowledge, union of forces is necessary."

Mayo WJ. The necessity of cooperation in the practice of medicine. *Collected Papers by the Staff of Saint Mary's Hospital, Mayo Clinic* 1910;2:557-566.

Dr. William J. Mayo, 1934

Dr. William J. Mayo, date of photograph unknown

"The advance in medicine has been so rapid that an enormous mass of undigested information has accumulated which we have had neither the time nor the perspective to analyze, to say nothing of correlating it with past experience, and the art of medicine has fallen behind the science."

Mayo WJ. The value of the imponderables in clinical medicine. Proceedings of the Inter-State Postgraduate Medical Assembly of North America, Cleveland, Ohio, October 16-21, 1933.

Dr. William J. Mayo with wife Hattie Damon Mayo and daughters Carrie and Phoebe, date of photograph unknown

"The relation of the physician to his patient is exceedingly close. The knowledge the physician obtains through confidential communications is kept inviolate. His associations with the family give him an understanding of their social, domestic, and financial conditions which is not equalled by that of the members of any other profession."

Mayo WJ. The value of the imponderables in clinical medicine. Proceedings of the Inter-State Postgraduate Medical Assembly of North America, Cleveland, Ohio, October 16-21, 1933.

"To books we turn to learn of the past, opinions of the present, and prognostications of the future."

Mayo WJ. Libraries useful in their day. *Bull Med Library Assoc* 1936;25:70-72.

The offices of Dr. William J. Mayo (top) and Dr. Charles H. Mayo (bottom) located in the Plummer Building, date of photographs unknown

"Instruction from teachers and books teaches a man what to think, but the great need is that he should learn how to think."

Mayo WJ. The establishment of the Mayo Foundation House and its purpose. *Proc Staff Meet Mayo Clin* 1938;13:553-554.

Dr. William J. Mayo, 1938

Dr. William J. Mayo and Dr. Charles H. Mayo, date of photograph unknown

"Medicine constantly became more complex. Year by year, more young physicians applied for positions as assistants and interns in the hospitals. The need of providing in some way a better form of graduate medical education for those earnest young men soon became apparent."

Mayo WJ. Sound recording, 1939.

"…possible influences that have contributed to the unusual growth of the clinic."

"…it would be natural to attribute the cause of their coming to work well done, but since good work is being done everywhere there must be another and deeper reason."

"Perhaps this other reason may best be summed up in one phrase, 'the spirit of the clinic' into which is incorporated the desire to aid those who are suffering, the desire to advance in medical education by research, by diligent observation, and by the application of knowledge gained by others and, most important of all, the desire to pass onto others the scientific candle this spirit has lighted."

Mayo WJ. Address of welcome. *Tr A Resid & Ex-Resid Physicians, Mayo Clin* 1919;1:16-17.

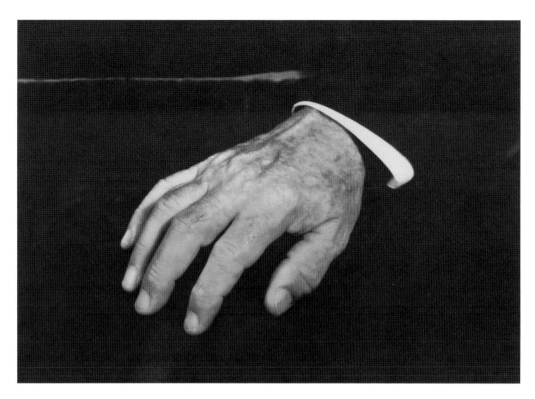

Dr. William J. Mayo's hand

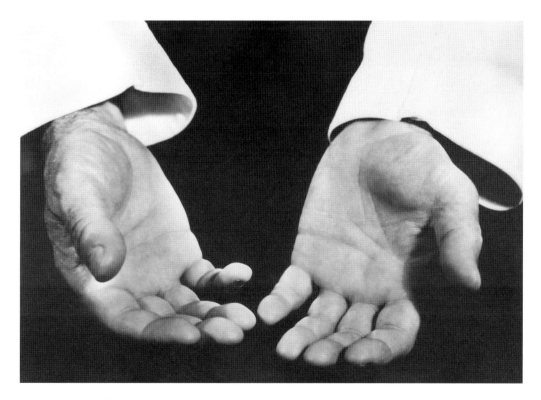

Dr. Charles H. Mayo's hands